QUICK GUIDE TO FANTASY BASKETBALL

by Brian Mahoney

BrightPoint Press

San Diego, CA

BrightPoint Press

an imprint of ReferencePoint Press, Inc.
Printed in the United States

For more information, contact:
BrightPoint Press
PO Box 27779
San Diego, CA 92198
www.BrightPointPress.com

LIBRARY OF CONGRESS CATALOGING-IN-PUBLICATION DATA

Names: Mahoney, Brian (Brian C.), author.
Title: Quick guide to fantasy basketball / by Brian Mahoney.
Description: San Diego, CA : ReferencePoint Press, [2021] | Series: Quick guide to fantasy sports | Includes bibliographical references and index. | Audience: Grades 10-12
Identifiers: LCCN 2020002434 (print) | LCCN 2020002435 (eBook) | ISBN 9781678200022 (Hardcover) | ISBN 9781678200039 (eBook)
Subjects: LCSH: Fantasy basketball (Game)--Juvenile literature.
Classification: LCC GV1202.F333 M35 2021 (print) | LCC GV1202.F33 (eBook) | DDC 793.93--dc23
LC record available at https://lccn.loc.gov/2020002434
LC eBook record available at https://lccn.loc.gov/2020002435

CONTENTS

AT A GLANCE

- In fantasy basketball, people put together teams of real-life NBA stars and earn points based on how those players perform.
- Fantasy basketball rules can be different from league to league.
- Fantasy basketball typically has two formats. In a season-long "roto" system, points are compiled over an entire season. In the head-to-head style, owners compete against each other every week.
- NBA teams play more than one game a week. Owners may need to change their lineups a few times a week.
- Owners have different strategies for building teams. They can try to have a balanced team, or they can focus on just being strong in a few categories.

- Owners can access great resources to help prepare. NBA statistics and fantasy tips and strategies are available on many websites. Owners need to look for ways to improve their teams by adding and dropping players.
- Players who are listed at multiple positions can have extra value.
- Trades can be difficult to make. But there are often better players available through trades.

GETTING THE WIN

Charlie was about to win a fantasy basketball championship. He had a big lead going into the final day. His friend, Casey, had Russell Westbrook playing. But how much difference could one player make? Plenty, as Charlie would learn.

Westbrook finished with twenty points, twenty rebounds, and twenty-one assists.

Getting involved in fantasy basketball makes watching NBA games more fun.

He was the second player in NBA history to have twenty in all three categories in a game. Westbrook's totals were unexpectedly high. Charlie was shocked. Casey managed to earn enough points to win.

Fantasy owners can't determine NBA team strategies, but they do control who is on their fantasy team.

FANTASY BASKETBALL BASICS

Fantasy basketball is about creating the best team. Participants, called owners, compete to have the most points, rebounds, and assists. Like a real NBA team, owners try to build a team with good shooting, size, and passing.

Players such as Westbrook, LeBron James, or James Harden do well in many areas. They can help a fantasy team win. But so can players who are good in only one area. Some players specialize in blocking shots or getting steals. These players are harder to find. With smart drafting and trades, an owner can become a champion.

The NBA has changed in recent years. Coaches say defense wins championships. However, offenses are thriving. Players are more skilled. The three-point shot is used more than ever. Teams scored more than 111 points per game in the 2018–19 season. That is ten more points per game than they averaged five years earlier. Basketball is looking better than ever. Fantasy basketball is a great way to enjoy it even more.

The Toronto Raptors won their first NBA championship in 2019.

CHAPTER ONE

WHAT IS FANTASY BASKETBALL?

In fantasy basketball, competitors create teams of NBA players. They manage the team just like a real NBA team.

Some players do amazing things. A powerful center could get twenty points. He could get twenty rebounds. A guard could have ten assists. He could make eight

Fantasy owners control their teams just like real NBA owners.

three-pointers. These performances are great to watch. They are especially fun for an owner who has those players.

"Imagine the feeling of having Stephen Curry on your squad when he has one of

Officials keep track of the game in many ways, including calling fouls and other rule violations on the court.

his classic shooting performances with ten three-pointers. Or what it feels like when reigning MVP Giannis Antetokounmpo erupts for a **triple-double** and adds three blocks to lead your team to victory," Joe Kaiser wrote on ESPN.com. "This stuff is a lot of fun!"[1]

LEARNING THE STATS

Every NBA game has officials. Some run up and down the court. They make calls. They can stop the game. Others sit behind computers. They track every player's movements. Every action gets recorded in a courtside computer. The officials record

Every action a player does on the court affects his box score.

when a player takes a shot. If the shot goes in, the player who passed it is credited with an assist. Whoever grabs a missed shot gets a rebound. Fouls and turnovers are

SIZING UP THE STATISTICS

What do good stats look like? The best scorers in the NBA average more than twenty-five points per game. Some average more than thirty. Other categories are much lower. The top rebounders usually average around fifteen. Assists are closer to ten. Blocks and steals are much lower. Someone who gets two per game would be among the best. Those are good numbers to keep in mind when picking players.

also entered. Defensive plays are tracked too. This includes blocked shots or stolen balls. The statistics are listed on the **box score**. Those totals form the basis of fantasy basketball. Owners earn points from these stats.

Points usually come from the same categories. They are scoring, rebounding, assists, field goal percentage, free throw percentage, three-pointers, blocks, and steals. Some leagues have a category for

LEBRON'S TRIPLE-DOUBLE THAT WASN'T

Fantasy performances aren't official without NBA approval. Some leagues give extra points for triple-doubles. LeBron James appeared to have one on February 4, 2009. He had fifty-two points, eleven assists, and ten rebounds. "I bet his fantasy owners are pretty happy," Cleveland teammate Wally Szczerbiak said. However, the NBA reviews all games. They determined James should not have received credit for one rebound. He lost the triple-double.

Quoted in Brian Mahoney, "LeBron's 50-Point Triple-Double Tops Knicks," NBC New York, *July 16, 2009. www.nbcnewyork.com.*

turnovers. That's the only category where the lowest score is best.

Giannis Antetokounmpo makes a basket after picking up a missed shot. This adds to a fantasy team's totals in three ways. He grabbed a rebound. Then he scored two points. Making a basket improved his field goal percentage too.

Field goal and free throw percentages are determined by the amount of shots a player makes. For field goals, NBA players want 50 percent or better. That means the player makes at least half the shots he takes. Nobody defends the shooter for free throws. That percentage should be higher. Players should be near 75 percent. That means they make three out of four shots.

Fans can guess the best players to have on a team. They are the players who can do many things. This is known as filling up the stat sheet. In basketball one player can make a major difference. A football team may have a great quarterback, but he cannot help its defense. Every baseball team wants an ace pitcher. However, few are strong hitters. NBA players play offense

No matter which type of league owners participate in, the goal is to get the most points.

and defense. They compile statistics on both ends of the floor.

Antetokounmpo finished in the top six in points and rebounds per game in 2018–19. He was voted the NBA's Most Valuable Player. That wasn't enough for his Milwaukee Bucks to win the championship. However, he helped all fantasy owners who drafted him.

TYPES OF LEAGUES

There are two main types of fantasy basketball. In the first, points are awarded over the entire season. If there are ten teams in the league, the team whose players grabbed the most rebounds gets ten points. The player with the fewest gets

A league's commissioner helps keep the league running smoothly.

The type of league can affect a fantasy team's performance.

one point. This continues for all of the categories. Then the scores are added. Whoever has the most points is the champion. A bad draft or an injury could cause a team to fall behind. It can be hard to catch up.

In other leagues, owners compete **head-to-head** each week. If there are nine categories, one player may have a higher total in six. If his opponent is better in the other three, the first player posts a 6–3 record that week. The top teams qualify for the playoffs. The winner of the playoffs is crowned champion. This type of league gives owners chances to get back on track after a slow start.

The disadvantage of head-to-head is that the best team might not win. One bad week at the wrong time could end an owner's championship hopes. A star player may be injured. Or he may only play two games during the matchup, while their opponent's best player has four games. Every NBA team plays eighty-two games. However, they don't all play the same number every week.

NBA players always want to have a high free throw percentage.

GETTING STARTED

A fantasy starting lineup includes guards, forwards, and a center. Some have a utility spot in the lineup, which can be filled by players who play any position. The leftover players are on the bench.

BEING COMMISSIONER

Being a commissioner may seem like a lot of work. However, many websites make it easy. Some websites can determine rules for a league. Many save customized league rules from previous seasons. Some websites will even serve as commissioner for the league. Leagues can also have co-commissioners to split the work.

Leagues can be very different. They decide the exact makeup of lineups. They also determine the scoring rules. It is important to know the league's rules. This way, an owner will know exactly what will help their team. Rules are usually determined by the **commissioner**. A commissioner is the person who has the power to make and enforce all league rules. Sometimes rules are decided by the website hosting the league. Once the rules are determined, it's time to prepare for the draft.

CHAPTER TWO

HOW DOES A PLAYER GET STARTED?

Paul George was drafted as a No. 10 pick. Kawhi Leonard was No. 15. Forty players were picked before Nikola Jokic in 2014. Somebody believed they would be great players, even when others didn't. An NBA manager's job is to find that type of player. They must put a strong team

An owner needs to predict which players will be the strongest in the upcoming season.

around him. This is what makes fantasy basketball so fun.

Fantasy basketball allows fans to do more than cheer for their favorite teams.

They prove how well they know basketball. They can turn their knowledge into a championship. But it takes work. The NBA season runs from October to April. There are games almost every night. In that way, fantasy basketball is tougher than football. In football, teams never play more than once a week.

An owner needs to know who is hot and who is not. This takes time and effort. “Fantasy basketball can be time-consuming and it takes practice and experience to excel. Winning your league for the first time

Successful owners follow the NBA teams their fantasy players are on.

WILL be worth it," Dicky Fung wrote on the basketball blog Off the Glass.[2]

JOINING A LEAGUE

There are opportunities to play all over the place. Someone could go from signing up to drafting a team in a matter of minutes. Many people play with their friends. They try to get together on draft night. They turn it into a party! It's fun to know one's competitors. But if not, it's still easy to play. Many sports websites operate fantasy leagues. Anyone can join one or more of them. All it takes is deciding what kind of league to play.

Fans of all ages can play fantasy basketball.

Someone who wants to be really involved might prefer a weekly head-to-head league. It requires having a lineup in place every

Many leagues turn draft day into a party to celebrate the start of the season.

night. Players injured in the middle of the week need to be replaced. Then they need to be put back in for the next game.

Owners follow the NBA teams their players are on. A player with only two games that week is usually not as valuable as one with four. More games means more chances to pile up statistics.

If that seems like too much work, owners may prefer a rotisserie format. These leagues are called roto for short. Points are added up over the entire season instead of week to week.

There are many different drafting styles. Owners can try which one seems best to them.

DRAFT DAY

Some leagues run their drafts using an **auction** format. Owners have the same amount of money to bid on players. They may decide to spend a lot of their budget on really good players. Then they fill out their roster with the little money they have

SEIZE THE THREES

Few players used to shoot three-pointers. Without drafting one early, it was hard to get a quality three-point shooter. Now, NBA teams sometimes try thirty to forty of these shots per game. That's good for fantasy owners. It's easier to find players who will help. However, opponents will too. "In any case," Alex Rikleen wrote on CBSSports.com, "these extra threes require some attention to make sure we are giving our teams the best chance at Fantasy success."

Alex Rikleen, "Fantasy Basketball: Three-Point Shooting Trend Watch Highlights Slow Starts for Stephen Curry, J.J. Redick," CBS Sports, *December 15, 2017. www.cbssports.com.*

left. Or, owners can try to use their money evenly and make a more balanced team.

Other leagues have owners take turns choosing players. Owners select one player when it's their turn. Most drafts use a **snake draft**. This means the owner with the last pick in each round gets the first pick in the next round. This continues until all the teams are full.

DRAFTING RESOURCES

Owners should come to the draft prepared. Many websites offer fantasy advice. Research is good for both experienced and new owners. Players are usually ranked

Checking stats online helps owners make informed draft decisions.

on the sites according to their statistics. Owners will have a good idea who they should try to draft first. Sites such as basketball-reference.com and NBA.com have detailed statistics. Owners can use these to predict which players will be the most valuable.

Fantasy basketball is not about picking favorite players. An NBA player who hustles

NBA PLAYERS AND FANTASY TEAMS

NBA players sometimes know they aren't just playing for their real teams. Harrison Barnes says fans have told him that he is on their fantasy squad. "All the time. You definitely hear that," he said. "Fans are like, 'Good luck tonight.'" He has an NBA title and an Olympic gold medal. He wants his owners to win too. "I try to do well for my team and the fans," he said.

Brian Mahoney. Interview with Harrison Barnes. November 3, 2019.

a lot and is a good teammate is easy to root for. He may even be a key player on the NBA team. Coaches like to call those players "glue guys." They help a team stick together. But without strong statistics, he won't help a fantasy team. When it comes to being the best in fantasy, numbers tell the story.

CHAPTER THREE

HOW IS A WINNING ROSTER BUILT?

Shaquille O'Neal was one of the league's dominant players. He stood 7-foot-1 and weighed 325 pounds. He was bigger and stronger than most players. Most couldn't stop his dunks or rebounds. He finished his career averaging 23.7 points and 10.9 rebounds.

Some players, such as Shaquille O'Neal, can be strong in some categories but weak in others.

Every player has weaknesses. Even superstars such as James Harden have at least one category they don't do well in.

However, Shaq wasn't a good free throw shooter. Most seasons he was around 50 percent. That meant he only made about half his shots. Some teams decided to foul him intentionally. This was known as "Hack-a-Shaq." They hoped he would miss the free throws. This was safer than risking him making a basket.

THE BEST IN SOME CATEGORIES

Shaq was great for points, rebounds, field goal percentage, and blocks. But he hurt fantasy teams in free throw percentage. There is no perfect player. Owners must plan when preparing for the draft. They will make hard decisions. Players who help in many categories can hurt in others.

Guards such as Stephen Curry and James Harden contribute a lot. They add points, three-pointers, and assists. But they often have a lot of turnovers. This is because they handle the ball more than others. Giannis Antetokounmpo is useful for scoring, rebounding, and field goal percentage. But three-pointers were his weakness when he was MVP. "If he starts hitting his threes at a better rate, he will be a consensus number one pick across

2019–2020 EXPERT DRAFT PICKS

RANK	ESPN PICK	FANTASY PROS PICK
1	Giannis Antetokounmpo (Milwaukee Bucks)	Anthony Davis (Los Angeles Lakers)
2	Karl-Anthony Towns (Minnesota Timberwolves)	Giannis Antetokounmpo (Milwaukee Bucks)
3	Anthony Davis (Los Angeles Lakers)	James Harden (Houston Rockets)
4	Nikola Jokic (Denver Nuggets)	Karl-Anthony Towns (Minnesota Timberwolves)
5	James Harden (Houston Rockets)	Stephen Curry (Golden State Warriors)
6	Stephen Curry (Golden State Warriors)	Nikola Jokic (Denver Nuggets)
7	LeBron James (Los Angeles Lakers)	Damian Lillard (Portland Trail Blazers)
8	Andre Drummond (Detroit Pistons)	Joel Embiid (Philadelphia 76ers)
9	Ben Simmons (Philadelphia 76ers)	Bradley Beal (Washington Wizards)
10	Pascal Siakam (Toronto Raptors)	LeBron James (Los Angeles Lakers)

Most fantasy resources offer rankings or suggestions on which players to draft. Names toward the top of the list tend to be more valuable players than those lower down. However, different experts offer different opinions. Some websites even give multiple rankings depending on the type of league. It is a good idea to compare the advice of many experts when preparing to draft your team.

all formats of fantasy basketball," Jason Bernard wrote on FantraxHQ.[3]

BALANCED OR UNBALANCED TEAMS?

Fantasy owners have to choose. They can assemble a balanced roster. They want to

PREPARE TO PASS THE TEST

Owners should look at the draft like a test. Without studying ahead of time, it may not go well. They make lists of players they want. When it's their turn to pick, they will know to choose the highest available one on their list. NBA teams prepare for their drafts for months. They rank players, see what they already have on their rosters, and check what they need. Fantasy owners should take drafts seriously too.

Owners want to be as prepared as possible for the draft. They should decide on their strategy ahead of time.

do well in many categories. They might get two good rebounders early. Then they draft players with other strengths with later picks.

Or, owners can choose a player like Shaq. They won't win the player's weakest category. They don't try to improve that category. Instead, they draft players with strengths in other categories. That team isn't very balanced. However, it might be more effective in some leagues.

Many coaches say that every NBA player is good. Some, however, are much better for fantasy teams. A good owner can identify those players. The best place

Owners should look for players who might be underrated and have the potential to do well. These players are easier to draft and can score many points.

to start is to study statistics. A player not producing big numbers isn't going to help a fantasy team.

There are other things to consider. Players listed at multiple positions are valuable. Someone may believe Joel Embiid is the NBA's best center. But if Embiid is only listed as a center, he can only be used in the center or utility positions. It might be better to draft a player listed as a center and forward. It is easier to put him in different spots. It helps avoid having to bench healthy players.

A player who can fill multiple positions can be more valuable than someone who can only fill one.

BOUNCE-BACK PLAYERS

Sometimes, players aren't coming off great seasons. But these players can be some of the best. See who had an injury. They may return to their normal level of play. This can benefit owners who take a chance. "By identifying bounce-back candidates, you may be able to get some steals in fantasy drafts in which other gamers are too hesitant to pull the trigger," Alex Barutha wrote on Yahoo Sports.[4] Also look for players gaining bigger roles on their teams.

A roster can be improved during the season. The draft is only the first step.

WHY DON'T HEALTHY PLAYERS ALWAYS PLAY?

Kawhi Leonard was the 2019 NBA Finals MVP. He was one of the league's best players. However, he sat out twenty-two games during the season. This was to keep him healthy. Leonard played only nine games in 2017–18 because of injuries. Owners know that healthy players don't always play. Check players' status daily. This is important, even if players aren't injured.

Owners note who was picked. They also see who wasn't. Some players who weren't drafted could become better than some who were. The best teams are built over an entire season. The right draft makes the work much easier.

CHAPTER FOUR

HOW DOES A FANTASY CHAMPIONSHIP BECOME REALITY?

On February 4, 2012, a little-known Knicks player named Jeremy Lin scored twenty-five points. His performance was surprising. He hadn't played much before. Lin wasn't sure he had a future with

Sometimes lesser-known players such as Jeremy Lin can step up and change the course of a season.

Sometimes a lesser-known player can strongly affect a fantasy team. These players are often called sleepers.

the NBA. Almost no fantasy owners drafted him. “He was on less than one percent of Americans’ fantasy basketball teams,” James Buckley Jr. noted in his book *Jeremy Lin: Rising Star*.[5]

After the game, coach Mike D’Antoni said Lin would become starting point guard. Point guards have earned great stats playing for D’Antoni. Steve Nash won two MVP awards under D’Antoni. Fantasy owners considered adding Lin. Those who did were quickly rewarded.

LINSANITY

Lin immediately put up big statistics. He had at least twenty points and seven assists in each of his first five starts. He scored 136 points. Lin was the first to reach those numbers since 1970. The excitement he created was called "Linsanity." But it didn't

OLD PLAYERS, NEW SKILLS

Owners looking to improve a category may get results from somebody they already have. That happens when players do something new. Take Brook Lopez, for example. He made only three three-pointers in his first eight seasons. Suddenly, he made 134 in 2016–17. An owner who drafted him expecting other strong categories got three-pointers too.

Injuries and bad seasons happen. Owners must be willing to change their teams to win.

last long. He hurt his knee in March. Lin needed surgery. He was out for the rest of the season. Owners dropped him after two months. Linsanity ended as suddenly as it began.

Those two months may have propelled a team toward a championship. Adding

AFTER LINSANITY

Jeremy Lin has not recaptured the excitement of Linsanity after the 2011–12 season. During his NBA career, Lin played for eight teams in nine seasons. In 2019, he became the first Asian American player to win a championship. However, he only averaged 3.4 minutes on the court during the playoffs. In 2019, Lin announced he would play in the Chinese Basketball Association for the Beijing Ducks.

players during the season can make a difference. It's rare for any team—real or fantasy—to win with its original roster. Owners must be flexible. Players get injured. They may not meet expectations. Don't worry if that happens. Teams can be improved. The team an owner drafts is rarely the one that ends the season.

FREE AGENTS

The easiest way to change a roster is by adding **free agents**. Owners should frequently check who isn't on a fantasy team. Sometimes those players become some of the best. Maybe a player was

Free agents can help teams earn more points and improve their standings.

injured and wasn't drafted. Or, someone may get more playing time. Owners should watch for those players. They should grab them before someone else.

In some leagues, free agents go to whoever who adds them first. Other leagues give owners an imaginary budget. They must spend that money to add a player.

Sometimes owners want a player dropped by another team. There is a **waiver process** to do this. The waiver process rules are determined by the league. Many leagues have similar rules. If more than one owner tries to add a player, he goes to the owner with the worst record so far that season.

MAKING TRADES

Another way to improve a team is through trades. An owner may notice that a rival has big men. They do well with rebounding but struggle in assists. The owner's own team has more assists, but the players fall short with rebounding.

A trade can solve both problems. One owner can propose a trade. This is a process where teams swap players. They can even exchange multiple players.

Both owners need to be happy about the deal being made during the trading process.

When a trade is offered, owners should have an honest discussion. “Listen to what the other player needs. Really listen. The only way this will work is if it’s a two-way conversation about what you both need and want,” Matthew Berry wrote on ESPN.com.[6]

Some owners don’t like trades. They worry a player they trade will suddenly play well. Don’t be surprised if a trade offer gets rejected. Trades often are approved by the commissioner. This makes sure the trade is fair. This protects the owners making the trade. It also is fairer for the rest of the league.

Just as in real sports, there is usually a trade deadline. This prevents an owner with no hope of winning from affecting teams who can. This keeps the end of the season fair.

FANTASY'S FINEST?

Fans often argue about the best NBA player. Many also argue over the best fantasy player. Experts agree it would have been hard to beat Wilt Chamberlain. The 7-foot-1 center had amazing statistics. In 1961–62, he averaged 50.4 points and 25.7 rebounds for the season! Chamberlain scored 100 points–an NBA record—and grabbed twenty-five rebounds on March 2, 1962. Fantasy website Draftkings.com determined that game would have been the best fantasy performance ever.

Trades can be more difficult than adding free agents. However, owners should try one. There may not be many strong free agents. Sometimes, a strong player is only gained by giving someone else up. Compromise is necessary. Adding and dropping players can feel like a lot of work. But, it will be worth it if it leads to a championship.

Fantasy basketball is a great way to engage with the sport in a new way. An owner will have to make tough choices. But he or she will gain new knowledge and

Tough decisions will pay off when a fantasy team does well.

spend time with friends. And of course, the champion gets to brag until next season.

GLOSSARY

auction

A draft where owners bid imaginary money for the players they want.

box score

Also called a stat sheet, it lists all the players' statistics in a game.

commissioner

The person who is in charge of making and enforcing the rules of a league.

free agents

Players who are not on any roster and are eligible to be added.

head-to-head

A league in which an owner competes against a different owner each week.

snake draft

A draft in which the owner with the last pick in the first round then chooses first in the second round.

triple-double

When a player has ten or more in three statistical categories.

waiver process

The way an owner can add a player who has been dropped off another team's roster.

SOURCE NOTES

CHAPTER ONE: WHAT IS FANTASY BASKETBALL?

1. Joe Kaiser, "ESPN Fantasy Basketball 101: How to Play," *ESPN.com*, September 24, 2019. www.espn.com.

CHAPTER TWO: HOW DOES A PLAYER GET STARTED?

2. Dicky Fung, "A Beginners Guide to Fantasy Basketball," *Off the Glass*. September 3, 2017. www.otgbasketball.com.

CHAPTER THREE: HOW IS A WINNING ROSTER BUILT?

3. Jason Bernard, "Rotisserie and Head to Head League Differences & Who to Avoid in Roto Leagues?" *Fantrax HQ*, August 7, 2019. www.fantraxhq.com.

4. Alex Barutha, "Fantasy Basketball: 14 Bounce-Back Candidates to Consider in Drafts." *Yahoo! Sports*, September 27, 2019. sports.yahoo.com.

CHAPTER FOUR: HOW DOES A FANTASY CHAMPIONSHIP BECOME A REALITY?

5. James Buckley Jr., *Jeremy Lin: Rising Star.* New York, NY: Scholastic Inc., 2012, p. 1.

6. Matthew Berry, "Love, Hate and How to Make a Trade," *ESPN.com*, October 2, 2019. www.espn.com.

FOR FURTHER RESEARCH

BOOKS

Matt Chandler, *Pro Basketball Records: A Guide for Every Fan*. North Mankato, MN: Compass Point Books, 2019.

Jeff Savage, *Basketball Super Stats*. Minneapolis, MN: Lerner Publications, 2017.

Dan Wetzel, *Stephen Curry*. New York, NY: Henry Holt & Company, 2019.

INTERNET SOURCES

Alex Barutha, "Fantasy Basketball: 14 Bounce-Back Candidates to Consider in Drafts," *Yahoo! Sports*, September 27, 2019. sports.yahoo.com.

Joe Kaiser, "ESPN Fantasy Basketball 101: How to Play," *ESPN.com*, September 24, 2019. www.espn.com.

Alex Rikleen, "Fantasy Basketball: Three-point Shooting," *CBSSports.com*, December 15, 2017. www.cbssports.com.

WEBSITES

Basketball Reference
www.basketball-reference.com

Basketball Reference is a website that covers a wide range of team, player, and game statistics.

NBA Fantasy and Gaming
www.nba.com/fantasy

NBA Fantasy and Gaming is the NBA's official fantasy basketball page. It includes fantasy analysis, player news, statistics, and other resources for fantasy owners.

Yahoo! Sports Fantasy
basketball.fantasysports.yahoo.com

Yahoo has a popular fantasy basketball league hosting service as well as breaking news and analysis from around the NBA.

INDEX

IMAGE CREDITS

Cover: © Matsuo K./Nippon News/Aflo Co. Ltd./Alamy
5: © Monkey Business Images/Shutterstock Images
7: © Yurdakul/iStockphoto
8: © Rawpixel.com/Shutterstock Images
11: © Frank Gunn/The Canadian Press/AP Images
13: © Wavebreakmedia/iStockphoto
14: © Aspen Photo/Shutterstock Images
16: © PhotoProCorp/Shutterstock Images
21: © Brocreative/Shutterstock Images
23: © Jakub Zak/Shutterstock Images
24: © kali9/iStockphoto
27: © Scott Meivogel/Shutterstock Images
31: © Mark J. Terrill/AP Images
33: © Kaspars Grinvalds/Shutterstock Images
35: © hedgehog94/iStockphoto
36: © fizkes/Shutterstock Images
38: © Chayantorn Tongmorn/Shutterstock Images
41: © franckreporter/iStockphoto
45: © Al Messerschmidt/AP Images
46: © Ross D. Franklin/AP Images
49: © Red Line Editorial
51: © FG Trade/iStockphoto
53: © SDI Productions/iStockphoto
55: © Chris Szagola/AP Images
59: © Jim Mone/AP Images
60: © Olena Yakobchuk/Shutterstock Images
63: © LightField Studios/Shutterstock Images
66: © TuelekZa/iStockphoto
69: © G-Stock Studio/Shutterstock Images
73: © g-stockstudio/iStockphoto

ABOUT THE AUTHOR

Brian Mahoney has been a national NBA writer for the Associated Press since 2005, covering the NBA Finals, All-Star Games, and international basketball events such as the Olympics and world basketball championships. Based in New York, where he lives with his wife and two daughters, Mahoney covers the Knicks and Nets, along with providing coverage of boxing and tennis events. He is a 1995 graduate of the University of Connecticut, where he started his career covering the women's basketball team that won the national championship. And yes, he has won a fantasy basketball championship.